vendor truck

tractor-trailer truck

straight truck

TRUCKS
BY GAIL GIBBONS

Harper & Row, Publishers

To Pat Allen and Barbara Fenton

Copyright © 1981 by Gail Gibbons
All rights reserved. Printed in the United States of America.
Published in hardcover by
Thomas Y. Crowell, New York

Library of Congress Cataloging in Publication Data
Gibbons, Gail.
Trucks.

Summary: Pictures a variety of trucks that work around us every day.
1. Trucks—Juvenile literature. [1. Trucks] I. Title.
TL230.G48   629.2'24   81-43039   AACR2
ISBN 0-690-04118-7   ISBN 0-690-04119-5 (lib. bdg.)
ISBN 0-06-443069-3 (pbk.)
First Harper Trophy edition, 1985.

Also by Gail Gibbons
Clocks and How They Go
Locks & Keys

pickup truck

logging truck

vendor truck

Bread

tank truck

al's

Trucks go everywhere—

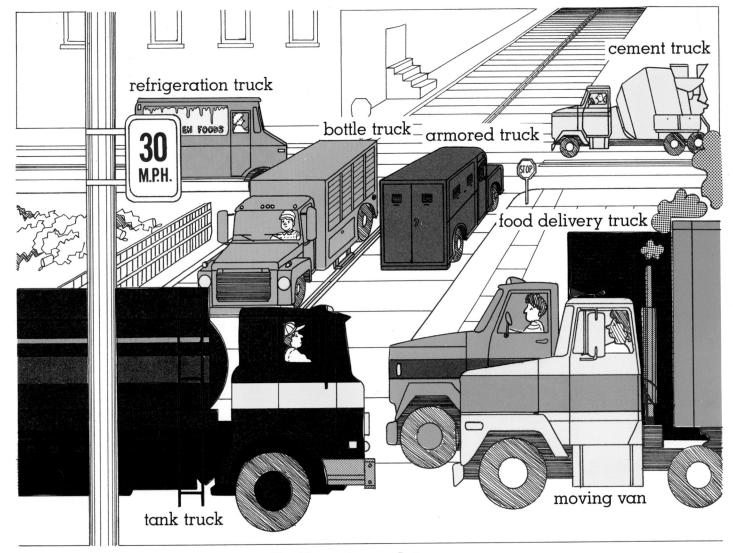

Delivering things,

tractor-trailer truck
carrying pickup trucks

Moving heavy loads,

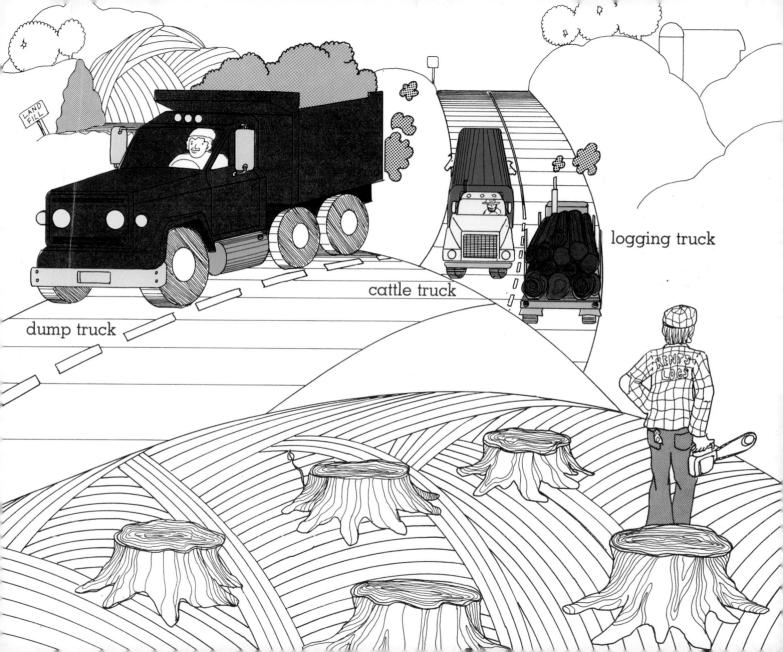

dump truck

cattle truck

logging truck

Pushing things,

tow truck

flatbed truck

HILL

Pulling things,

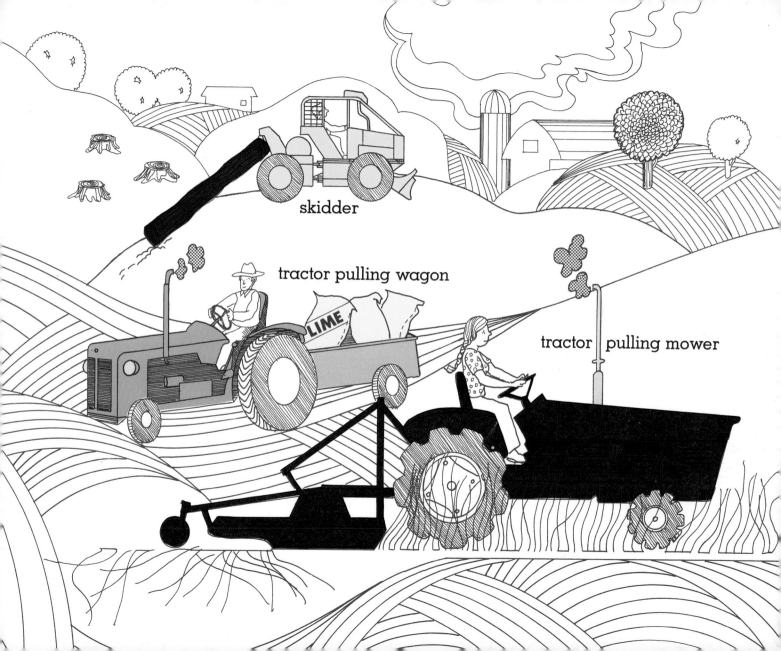

skidder

tractor pulling wagon

LIME

tractor pulling mower

small crane

OAKES LUMBER

payloader

Lifting things, too.

power grapple

cherry picker truck

forklift truck

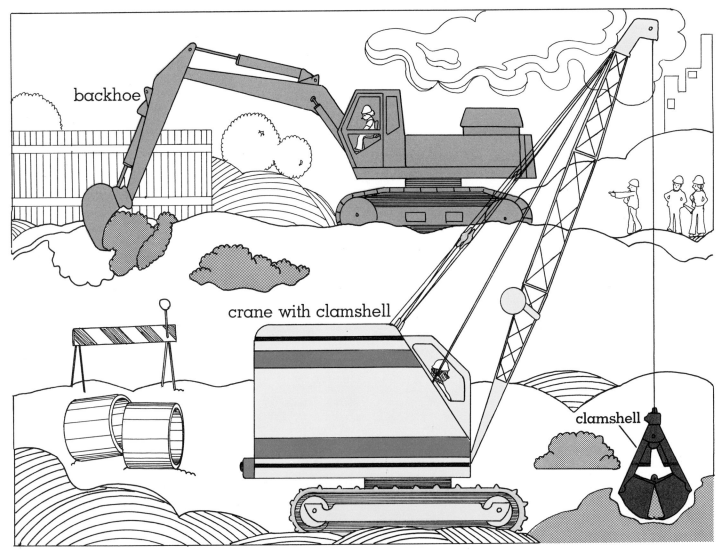

backhoe

crane with clamshell

clamshell

Trucks dig holes.

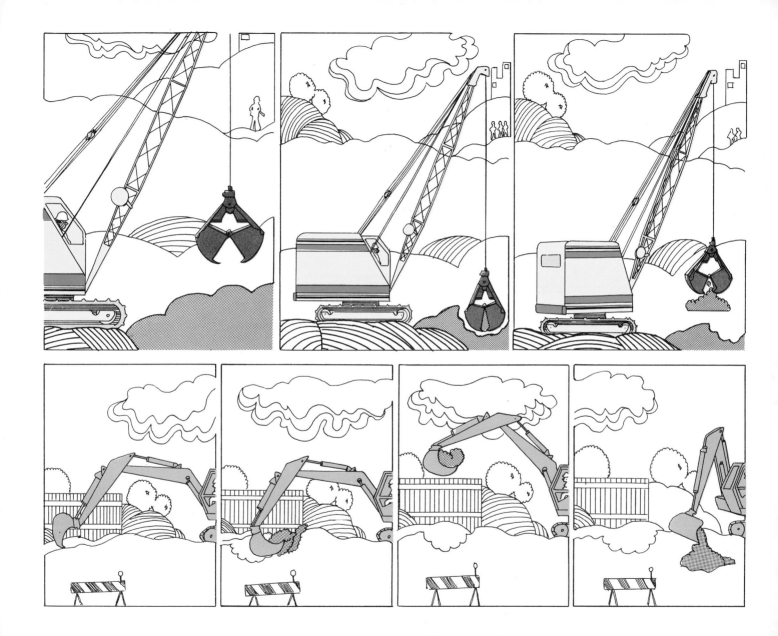

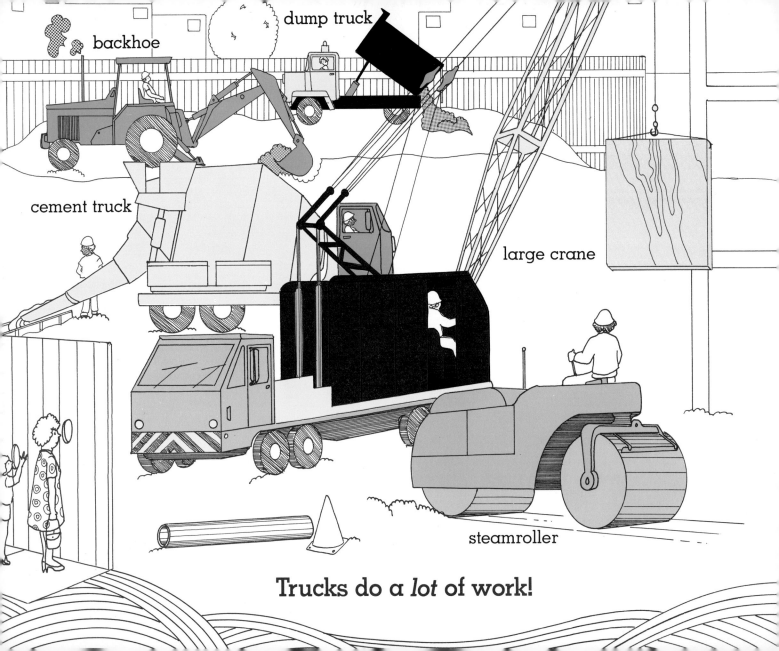

backhoe

dump truck

cement truck

large crane

steamroller

Trucks do a *lot* of work!

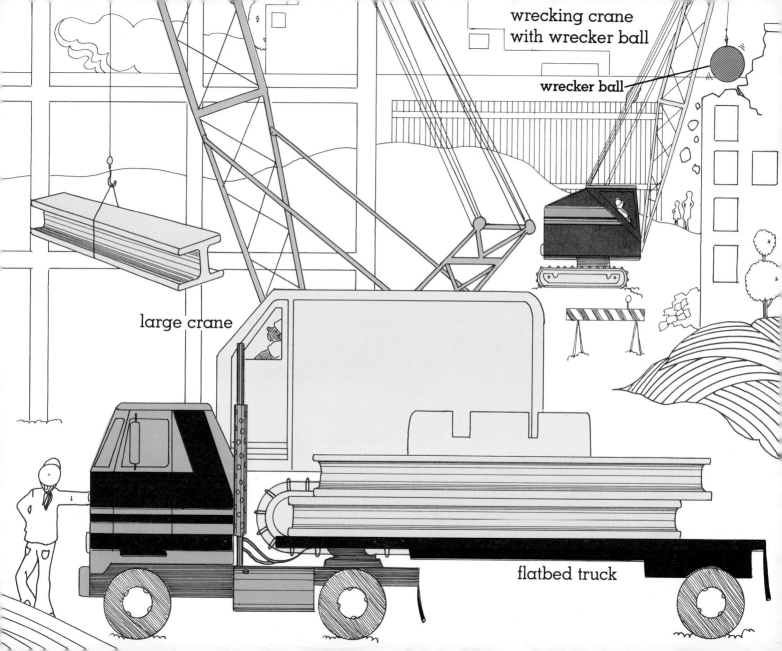

wrecking crane
with wrecker ball

wrecker ball

large crane

flatbed truck

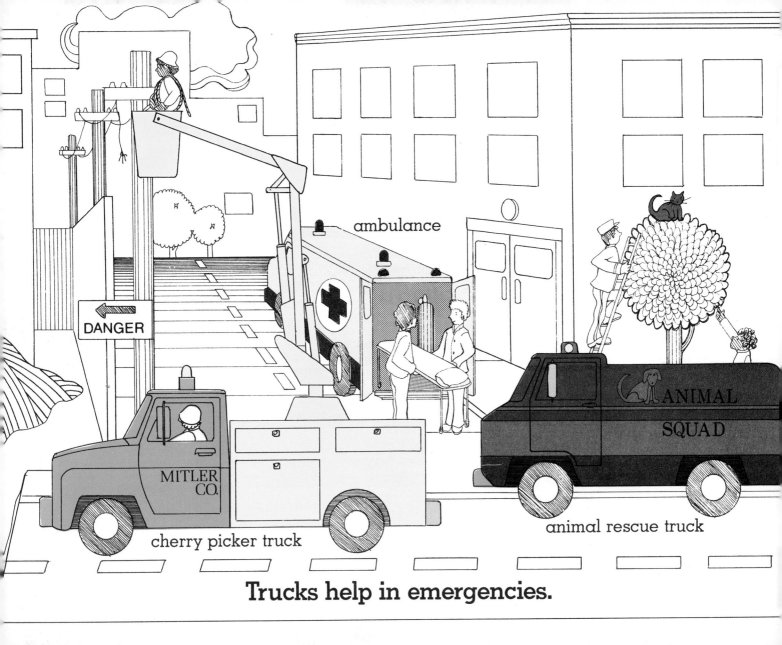

DANGER

ambulance

MITLER CO.

ANIMAL SQUAD

cherry picker truck

animal rescue truck

Trucks help in emergencies.

police rescue
truck

fire truck

tow truck

ERIC SERVICE

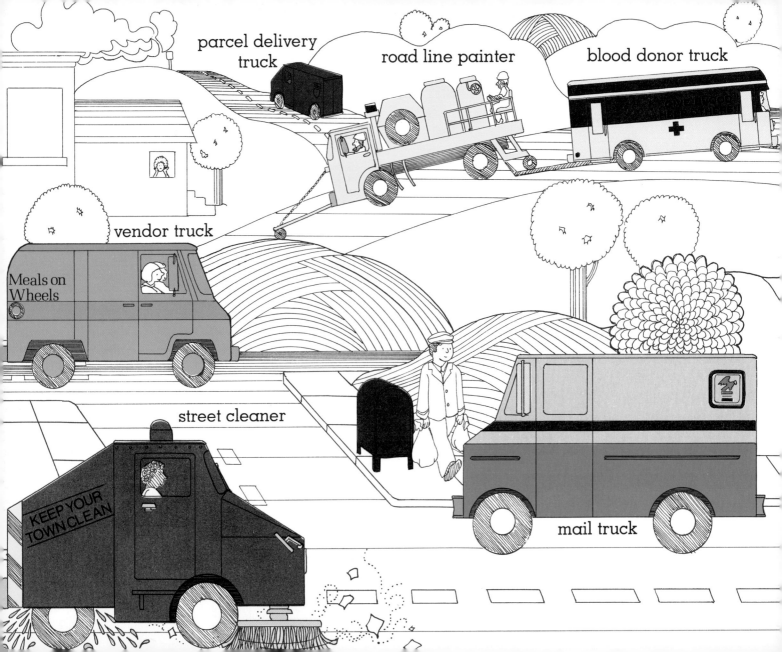

parcel delivery truck

road line painter

blood donor truck

vendor truck

Meals on Wheels

street cleaner

KEEP YOUR TOWN CLEAN

mail truck

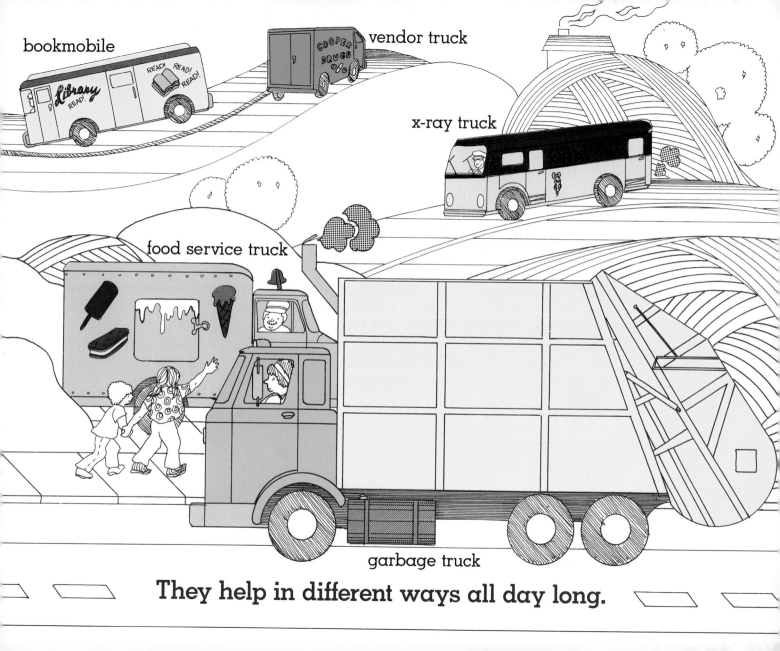

bookmobile

vendor truck

x-ray truck

food service truck

garbage truck

They help in different ways all day long.

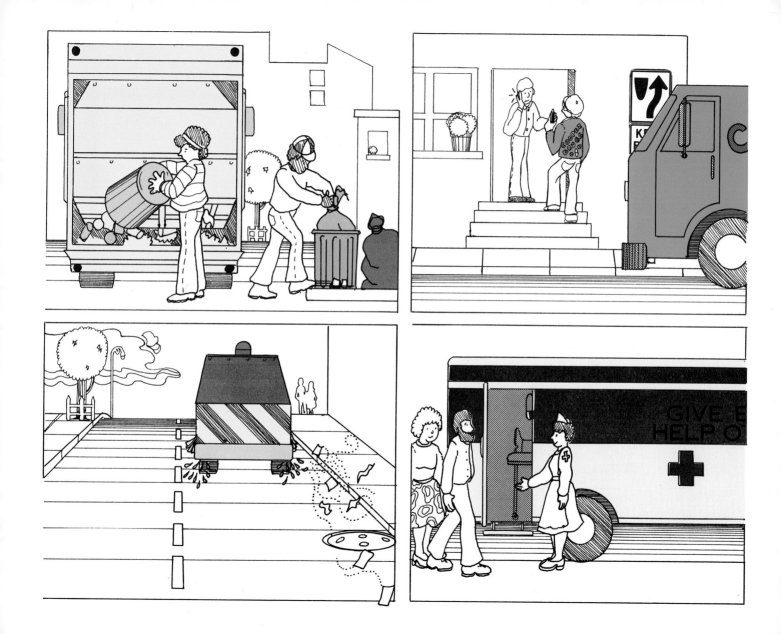

Everywhere you look—trucks on the move.

The Parts of a Truck

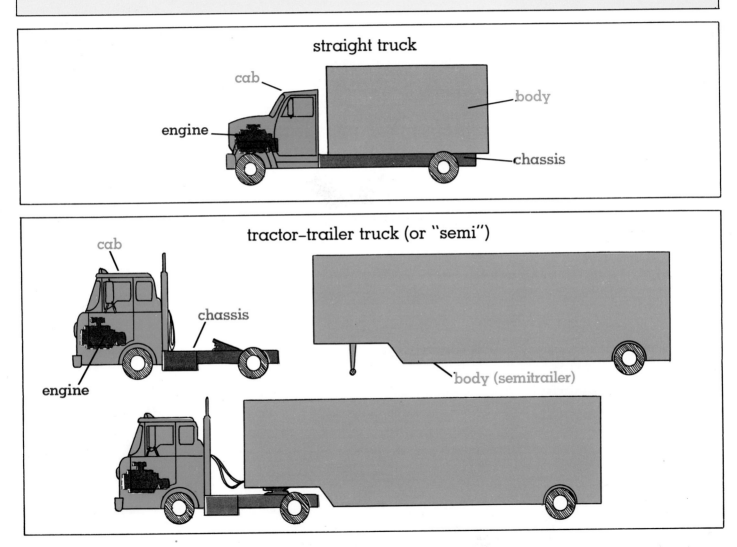

straight truck

cab

engine

body

chassis

tractor-trailer truck (or "semi")

cab

chassis

engine

body (semitrailer)